Discovering the "Awe"
of the Mass

Discovering the "Awe" of the Mass

by Regis J. Flaherty

EMMAUS
ROAD
PUBLISHING

Steubenville, Ohio
A Division of Catholics United for the Faith
www.emmausroad.org

EMMAUS
ROAD
PUBLISHING

Emmaus Road Publishing
827 North Fourth Street • Steubenville, Ohio 43952

Library of Congress Control Number: 2012944246
ISBN: 9781937155834

Cover design and layout by Julie Davis, General Glyphics, Inc., Dallas, Texas
(www.glyphnet.com)

Nihil Obstat: Rev. Joseph J. Kleppner, STL, PhD, Censor Librorum,
Diocese of Pittsburgh
Imprimatur: Most Rev. David A. Zubick, DD, Bishop of Pittsburgh
December 15, 2009

To my mother, Rosemary Flaherty,
who not only introduced me to the Catholic Faith
but also continues to teach me
through her example of faithfulness and virtue.

Contents

Introduction

There are (or there should be) those "awe" occasions in everyone's life—those times when the situation, place, or event leaves us, as it were, breathless. When we are overcome by the beauty, grandeur, or holiness of the moment. Witnessing the birth of my first child was one such occasion for me. I didn't know whether to laugh, or cry, or just drop to my knees. Surely all were appropriate.

And I still remember the feeling when I stepped close enough to see the panorama of the Grand Canyon. I experienced the grandeur of creation and the glory of God at a depth I had not previously known. It left me speechless (no mean feat for a man who makes his living working with words).

Mass is an "awe" event, and we should experience some of that awe as we participate in the liturgy. But for many of us that is not our experience.

1

We are often tempted to define a "good" Mass by the externals: the quality of the music, the participation of the congregation, the beauty of the sanctuary or vestments, the delivery of the homily. Those items are important—we should strive for beauty and reverence—and they can help us appreciate the Mass. Nonetheless, the Mass, even when celebrated in the dingiest environment, with a monotone voiced priest, no music, and half of the congregation asleep, is, in its reality, still an "awe" experience.

This booklet examines the Mass in order to deepen the "awe" that we should experience each and every time we attend the liturgy. This appreciation is enhanced by an increase of knowledge and understanding. However, more important than information is *heart* formation. That latter activity is dependent on the Holy Spirit and our openness to His activity. So I suggest you start your reading—as I start my writing—with a prayer. Use your own words or mine:

> *Divine and Holy Spirit, I know that the Mass*
> *is a great gift to the Church and to me in par-*
> *ticular. I know it is meant to nourish me and*

bring me closer to You in the Trinity. I begin to read now with the desire to enhance my understanding of the Mass. Open my mind to Your truth. Open, too, my heart to the work that You want to do in me. Divine Paraclete, guide me in the ways of truth and to a closer relationship with You, the Father, and the Son. Amen.

Overview of the Mass

To appreciate the awe of the Mass we need something more than our five physical senses. We need to view the Mass with spiritual eyes. We must see the reality behind the externals. So, please, take a walk with me through the Mass, using the Catechism of the Catholic Church as a guide. Let's look at the Eucharistic Liturgy through spiritual lenses. Be careful—it may just take your breath away.

Introductory Rites

All Gather Together (CCC 1348)

As we start down the aisle to find a seat for Mass, most of us will dip our fingers into the water of a font. In Baptism blessed water was poured over our heads and we were baptized in "the name of the Father, and of the Son, and of the Holy Spirit." With those words and actions a profound and permanent change occurred. We were brought into God's family. So, those few drops that we place on our forehead as we enter church harken back to that water of Baptism. We make the Sign of the Cross with the same Trinitarian formula that claimed us for God at Baptism. We are not strangers. We are God's children and we come by invitation.

As we move toward a seat, we perform another action. We genuflect—an act of reverence and submission. It is not a common practice in our culture, but appropriate when we consider to whom we genuflect. We bend our knee to acknowledge and worship Jesus, truly present in the Eucharist reserved in the tabernacle. (You can tell that He is there if a candle or light, usually red, is lit next to the tabernacle.) When we genuflect, it is an opportunity to recollect. We might have rushed from home or we may have many practical matters on our minds, but that genuflection is an opportunity to stop and focus. Jesus is here. I submit myself to Him. I turn my heart and my mind to the Savior of the world.

"I rejoiced because they said to me, 'We will go up to the house of the Lord.' And now we have set foot within your gates" (Ps. 122:1–2, NAB). Those words of the psalmist come from one of the Songs of Ascent, sung by the Israelites as they processed to the Temple in Jerusalem. They are apt words for us as we begin the Eucharistic celebration. As the priest processes up the aisle, we usually sing a hymn, as is befitting. Joy and praise should accompany any celebration, and this is no ordinary celebration. *God* is coming!

Mass begins as the celebrant and attendants process to the altar. Physically we may not be in that procession but we are to participate spiritually. The crucifix, carried by an altar server, passes us in the procession—the Cross that Saint Paul calls "the power of God and the wisdom of God" (1 Cor. 1:24). It reminds us that salvation and life is offered to us. Called away from our daily routine, it is an eternal reality that beckons us to stand and rejoice. We have entered the house of God—encountering a reality even more profound than the one the Israelites found in the Temple.

The priest and deacon wear special clothing, called vestments. This garb, or at least clothing similar to it, was typical dress in the time of the early Church. The vestments point back to the time of our Lord and to that first Mass. But that ancient garb also reminds us that what happened so many centuries ago happens again today, in this church in which we gather.

Wipe Your Feet

Before you come as a guest into someone's home, you will probably bathe, groom, and put on appropriate clothing. We have been invited to the banquet feast of the Lamb of God. We should come ready. Surely that means some physical preparation, cleaned and appropriately clothed, but we also remember that in the Mass we are dealing with realities beyond what our eyes can see. There is a spiritual cleansing to which we should attend before we arrive at Mass. If we have unconfessed serious sin, that which is called *mortal*, on our conscience, we should confess it in the Sacrament of Reconciliation before coming to the table of our Lord. Scripture tells us that it is a serious sin to partake of the Body and Blood of the Lord unworthily. (If someone is aware of an unconfessed mortal sin, he or she should not receive Communion until making a sincere confession in the Sacrament of Reconciliation. See 1 Corinthians 11:29.)

However, even if we have bathed, groomed, and dressed, we will still pick up a degree of dust and dirt as we travel to the home to which we have been invited. Most likely our shoes will be somewhat soiled. So, as we enter the house, we wipe our feet. That dirt isn't enough to keep us from coming, but wiping our feet before we enter is something that we do so as not to bring dirt into the house of the host.

At the beginning of each Mass we have the opportunity to "wipe our feet" during the "penitential rite." This is not a replacement for the Sacrament of Reconciliation, but it does take care of some stains on our souls—*venial* sins—perhaps from times we failed to act as we should, or had sinful thoughts. The priest reminds us: "Let us call to mind our sins." "Lord, have mercy," we pray—and He *is* merciful. In fact, it is He who cleanses us, just as He washed the feet of His first disciples at that first Eucharist on a Thursday during the Jewish Passover.

I Confess

The Penitential Rite can take several forms. One involves the recitation of the Confiteor (that is, "I confess"). Anyone who was an altar boy when the Mass was said in Latin will remember that when the server said the Confiteor, at the words "mea culpa," he would strike his breast with his right hand. When vernacular was introduced, the Confiteor was maintained as an option for the penitential rite, but that striking of the chest at the words "through my fault" was dropped. More recently, it has been reintroduced.

Those who watch sports are familiar with this gesture. If the shortstop overthrows the first baseman or the point guard makes a turnover, the player will point to his or her chest and mouth the words "my fault." But why bother? Everyone knows which player erred. Yet the player makes the gesture to accept responsibility for his action. In this action there is an unspoken promise to do better next time.

When the priest encourages us to call to mind our sins we remember the words of Saint Paul: "All have sinned and fall short of the glory of God" (Rom. 3:23). We also know that we need to be accountable. The penitential rite gives us the opportunity to admit our sinfulness and to ask God to forgive our venial sins before we enter into the liturgy. The striking of the breast, similar to the action of the ballplayer, makes an important statement. It is *I* who has sinned. I have offended God.

And it is I who has weakened the community of believers. True, we are all sinners, but admitting my personal responsibility is a required first step both for forgiveness and for making improvements. With humility and true sorrow I publicly strike my breast—my heart—and admit my personal sin, asking a merciful God to grant forgiveness so that I may enter into the celebration of the Mass and be fed with the Bread of Life.

Glory to God

After the penitential rite we normally recite the "Gloria." This prayer of praise does contain petitions: "Have mercy on us" and "Receive our prayer." However, the requests are presented in an atmosphere of hope. God does "take away the sins of the world." Jesus, our intercessor, is "seated at the right hand of the Father." In fact, the Gloria that we pray begins with the words that angels proclaimed more than two thousand years ago as they announced to shepherds the birth of the Savior (see Lk. 2:14). Truly, He is intercessor, savior, and the reason for a confident hope.

Liturgy of the Word

After a short prayer appropriate to the liturgical celebration of the day, we begin the Liturgy of the Word (see CCC 1349).

Words can convict or heal; words can bring light or confusion; they can seal a promise or convey a lie. Words are powerful, but mere mortal words pale before the reality and power of God's Word. When God spoke at the beginning of time, creation occurred. God's Word, spoken in the Old Covenant, formed, directed, and preserved God's people, the nation of Israel. God's Word is still at work today.

Some words are more valuable than others. When a wise man speaks, it's worth listening. If someone trustworthy gives a guarantee, we have confidence in the transaction. God stands behind His Word. It is the truth backed by power. When God made covenants (remember Adam and Eve,

Abraham, Jacob, Moses, David, etc.), He always kept His Word, even though His people seldom kept their promises.

Many Scriptures speak about the nature and power of God's Word. For example:

> *For the word of God is living and active, sharper than any two-edged sword, piercing to the division of soul and spirit, of joints and marrow, and discerning the thoughts and intentions of the heart. (Heb. 4:12)*

> *All scripture is inspired by God and profitable for teaching, for reproof, for correction, and for training in righteousness, that the man of God may be complete, equipped for every good work. (2 Tim. 3:16–17)*

Now consider: we receive God's Word at each and every Mass. When we take a moment to recognize that God speaks to us through Scripture, surely only one word is fitting: "Awesome!"

To hear God's Word, we must actively listen. On several occasions Jesus said: "He who has ears, let him hear" (Mt. 13:9; Mt. 11:15; Mk. 4:9; cf. Mk. 4:23; Ps. 78:1). We need spiritual ears that are attuned, not only to words, but also to the Holy Spirit who speaks them.

How can we open our spiritual ears to better hear? First, knowing the power of God's Word, we should be expectant. As the Scriptures point out, God's Word can recreate, heal, convict, equip—make us into the men and women we are meant to be.

To hear we need to stop speaking and be quiet—quieting not only our lips, but our mind and spirit as well. God is speaking to us through His Word, and we need to put everything else aside so that we can receive. Yet, listening is not a passive activity—quite to the contrary. The interior quieting must be accompanied by an *active* listening. As we turn away from distractions, we are to consciously turn to God. A prayer to the Holy Spirit is appropriate as we prepare to hear the Scripture proclaimed. It was He who inspired the evangelists and it is He who can open our ears to receive God's Word.

To help our hearing it is also a good practice to read the Sunday readings (Old Testament, New Testament, Psalm response, and Gospel) before attending Mass. Ask our good God to show you what He is saying to you through those Scriptures.

Before we hear the Gospel proclaimed, we sing an "alleluia acclamation." This is the same acclamation that Saint John tells us is sung in heaven before the throne of God (see Rev. 19). It is the joyful shout of God's people to the coming of the Word of God.

As the priest moves toward the ambo (lectern) to read the Gospel, he pauses and bows to the altar whispering, "Cleanse my heart and my lips, Almighty God, that I may worthily proclaim your holy gospel."* When the priest arrives at the ambo, he speaks to the congregation: "The Lord be with you." He then proclaims, "A reading from the holy gospel according to …" and with his thumb makes a small Sign of the Cross on the book and, then, on his forehead, lips, and chest. We too make the triple sign, professing faith and, perhaps, silently praying, "Lord, may Your Word be in my thoughts, on my lips, and in my heart."

---

* If a deacon assists at Mass, he will proclaim the Gospel. Before going to the ambo the deacon will bow before the priest and request his blessing. The celebrant will then pray: "May the Lord be in your heart and on your lips that you may proclaim his gospel worthily and well…"

The priest or deacon will give a homily after the reading of the Gospel. This is mandated on Sundays and holidays, and encouraged at daily Mass. The homily can only be given by an ordained minister—bishop, priest, or deacon. Preaching is part of the responsibility and the gift given to the priest at his ordination. He represents Christ the Teacher and Shepherd (CCC 1548).

I Believe

We have arrived at a hinge moment of the Mass. We have opened our hearts and minds to the Holy Spirit and have listened to the Scriptures and the words of the priest, Christ's minister. We are almost ready to begin the Liturgy of the Eucharist, the central liturgical event of our faith.

We are stirred to action. God has *spoken* to us. God has spoken to *me*. When God spoke in Genesis, the world and all that is in it was created. At Christ's word miracles occurred—the blind gained sight, cripples walked, waves calmed, and people rose from the dead! Now He has spoken to all at Mass—indeed, this is a jaw-dropping moment when seen with the eyes of faith.

What is the appropriate response? *I believe!* We stand and together proclaim the Profession of Faith.[†] Recall the words of Peter when Christ asked him, "Who do you say that I am?" Peter replied, "You are the Christ, the Son of the living God" (Mt. 16:15–16). This occurred at a pivotal time—a hinge time—for Peter. He had been following Jesus, hearing His teaching, and witnessing His work. What was coming was the reason for Jesus' life—that final dinner with His disciples, and His suffering, death, and Resurrection. Peter needed to stand and profess his faith in Jesus so to enter into the Paschal Mystery.

It is the same for us at this pivotal time in the Mass. We believe and we too are ready to share in His Paschal Mystery—the Eucharist which partakes of that same supper, that same crucifixion, and that same Resurrection.

---

† Also called the Creed.

Liturgy of the Eucharist

The Offertory

The movement of the Mass now takes a turn. The Scriptures have been proclaimed and expounded upon in the sermon, and we have professed our faith. After the "Prayer of the Faithful" (also called the General Intercessions), the Liturgy of the Word ends and the Liturgy of the Eucharist begins with the presentation of the bread and wine, or the *Offertory* (see CCC 1350).

We neither come to Mass empty-handed nor with empty hearts. We bring our God-given talents, our concerns, our confusion, our hopes, our faults, our fears, our struggles—we bring our often troubled lives with us. We bring the good and the not so good. But no matter the state of our lives, we can come with confidence. Remember what Jesus said? "Let the children come to me" (Mt. 19:14), and through our baptism we have become His dear children. He invites those who are "heavy laden" to come and find rest (Mt. 11:28).

Recall the actions of Jesus described in the Gospel of Matthew. Two thousand years ago on a hill in Israel, Christ invited the multitude who had been following Him to sit, and He fed them—Matthew tells us it was five thousand men not counting women and children—with a few loaves of bread that were offered to Him (see Mt. 14:14–21).

After hearing Christ's teaching in the Liturgy of the Word, we too are invited to sit, offer what we have, and allow Him to work a miracle. At Mass, Christ again wants to feed the "gathered multitude" and He looks for our offering. Bread and wine are brought forward: simple food and drink that, through the action of Jesus, will feed us with abundance that is beyond our imagination.

When that bread and wine are brought forward, we are encouraged to add the gift of ourselves to the offering. We offer what we have brought; we offer Him our lives, as they are. It does not take many words. Perhaps we simply say in the depths of our heart: "Lord, my life to you, your life to me." In fact, words are secondary; an act of the will and a movement of the heart are required. We come with a spiritual hunger, knowing that He, who has fed so many, will also feed us.

Not for Us Alone

God's work is not limited only to those in attendance at this particular Mass. The triumph of Calvary and the grace of the Eucharist can reach and bless others. So the priest may offer Mass for the intention of some individual(s), living or deceased. We too can bring someone along with us to Mass but not necessarily physically. When we offer ourselves with the bread and wine, we can bring those for whom we pray—perhaps a parent, a spouse, a child, a friend in need. We can offer to God that person who is on our heart and mind, with a prayer that the grace of the Mass reaches them as well.

Then, when the priest lifts the paten containing the offered bread, our lives, intentions, and needs can be in that offering. Indeed, as the priest prays in the Eucharistic Prayer, "It will become for us the bread of life."

The priest then adds a drop of water to the wine already poured into the chalice; we again see that in this action we are added to the offering of wine. The priest prays, "By the mystery of this water and wine may *we* come to *share* in the divinity of Christ" (emphasis added).

With a bow to the altar containing the gifts we offer, the priest prays for those gathered: "With humble spirit and contrite heart may we be accepted by you, O Lord, and may our sacrifice in your sight this day be pleasing to you, O God."

And when the priest soon invites us to "pray, brethren, that my sacrifice and yours may be acceptable to God, the almighty Father," we stand and we do pray: "May the Lord accept the sacrifice." It is bread; it is wine; it is you; and it is me. We give the offering first for the "praise and glory" of our Savior, but also "for our good and the good of all his Church."

The Preface (CCC 1352)

We then stand, acknowledging another shift in the Mass. Our focus up until now has been primarily on ourselves. We confessed our sinfulness, heard the Word, and offered our gifts. Now we must forget ourselves for we are preparing to behold the greatest wonder of the world. We will behold a miracle that makes the birth of a first child, the vastness of the Grand Canyon, indeed the glory of the created universe pale in comparison.

The priest will recite a prayer, the Preface (see CCC 1352), that changes somewhat depending on the liturgical season—Lent, Easter, the commemoration of a saint, the feast day of our Lord or our Lady, and so on. These prayers all start the same: "Father, all-powerful and ever-living God, we do well always and everywhere to give you thanks." The prayer then gives us a reason for giving thanks. That reason is tied to the liturgical calendar.

As we listen to the Preface, we turn our eyes to God and to Him alone. The priest finishes his prayer by inviting all present to sing praises to God "with all the choirs of angels."

Singing with the Angels

It is now our turn to respond to the call—to sing with the choirs of angels!

When we look around the church and listen with our physical ears, we don't see or hear angels. Instead, we see the person sitting in front of us and the woman with the oddly colored coat across the aisle. We hear the priest, as well as the cough of the old man and the cry of the baby. However, at Mass there is more to see and hear than what meets the eye or tickles the ear. We must be careful because our physical eyes and ears can deceive us. There are sights and sounds that require an inner vision and spiritual hearing to appreciate. While we are at Mass, something is happening in heaven:

Day and night they never cease to sing, "Holy, holy, holy, is the Lord God Almighty, who was and is and is to come!" And whenever the living creatures give glory and honor and thanks to him who is seated on the throne, who lives for ever and ever, the twenty-four elders fall down before him who is seated on the throne and worship him who lives for ever and ever; they cast their crowns before the throne, singing, "Worthy art thou, our Lord and

God, to receive glory and honor and power, for thou didst create all things, and by thy will they existed and were created." (Rev. 4:8–11)

While remaining at our pew we are called to participate in what continues in the heavenly kingdom. With our spiritual eyes we realize that the archangels, the cherubim, the seraphim, and all the saints who have gone before us invite us to their church—into their worship service. They are singing "Holy, holy, holy" to the King of kings. When we sing our "Holy, holy, holy" we are merely joining the song already in progress.

Those saints are in such awe that they "fall down before" Christ enthroned in glory. If we adjust our spiritual vision, we too will be in awe.

The Eucharistic Prayer

The priest then begins one of the several Eucharistic Prayers. Each has a distinct beauty. For example, Eucharistic Prayer I is known as the "Roman Canon" and sounds most familiar to older Catholics who remember the pre-Vatican II Mass.

Eucharistic Prayer II is short but has beauty in its simplicity.

All of the Eucharistic prayers begin by addressing God the Father. It is the "Father . . . who has blessed us in Christ with every spiritual blessing" (Eph. 1:3).*

The Epiclesis (CCC 1353)

Each and every one of the Eucharistic prayers contains a short prayer, the Epiclesis, which the priest says with his hands extended over the elements of the offering. This prayer invokes the Holy Spirit, asking Him to bless the gifts "that they may become for us the Body and Blood of our Lord, Jesus Christ." In some churches bells are rung. They compliment the words and remind us that Christ is near. We want to be attentive.

---

* Reading the first chapter of Ephesians gives a good summary of what the Father has done for us in Christ.

The Institution Narrative (CCC 1353)

The Mass is truly a Trinitarian event. At this point in the Liturgy of the Eucharist the Father has been addressed and the Holy Spirit invoked. Now Christ, through the priest, speaks the "words of institution"—also called the Consecration. Over the bread we hear Christ's words, "This is my Body which will be given up for you." Over the wine we hear, "This is the chalice of my Blood, the blood of the new and eternal covenant." How often have we heard those words? How deeply have we grasped their meaning? The Catechism tells us, "it is by the conversion of the bread and the wine into Christ's Body and Blood that Christ becomes present" (1375).

We must pause. Awe demands it. The priest holds up for us the Host, which no longer is bread, and the chalice, which no longer contains wine. This miracle is called *transubstantiation*. The whole substance of the bread and wine becomes the Body and Blood of Christ (CCC 1376). Only the appearances of bread and wine remain.

Those words of Christ, spoken at the Last Supper and repeated at every Mass, are intimately tied to His crucifixion. The two constitute one and the same sacrifice. We kneel at the foot of the Cross of Calvary at each Mass. Christ does not die again; rather, the veil of time is torn asunder and we enter into something eternal.

When Saint John saw his heavenly vision, as recorded in the Book of Revelation, he beheld the "Lamb, standing, as though it had been slain" (Rev. 5:6). Jesus is that Lamb, and His sacrifice speaks for us before the throne of His Father forever. Though still earthbound, at each Mass we enter into something eternal. Our earthly eyes can't see the mystery. But Scripture gives us a glimpse of what occurs at the arrival of the sacrificed Lamb, Jesus, in heaven.

Those in heaven "fell down before the Lamb." "Bowls full of incense" representing the prayers of the saints are offered in His honor. And it is not a quiet gathering: "The voice of many angels, numbering myriads of myriads and thousands of thousands, saying with a loud voice, 'Worthy is the Lamb who was slain'" (Rev. 5:8, 11–12).

We, too, kneel before the same Lamb present on the altar. The priest proclaims the great reality: "The mystery of faith." And we have an opportunity to join the heavenly chorus as we respond: "We proclaim your death, O Lord, and profess your Resurrection until you come again."

The Anamnesis and the Intercessions (CCC 1354)

After the Consecration—as though we realize that we are not alone and that this sacrifice is given for the benefit of all men—the priest prays for the living and the dead, for those present, and for the pope, the bishop, and the clergy. We too can again remember those for whom we pray in particular at this Mass. As the priest prays, we are reminded of those who see this sacrifice most intimately, the saints, including Mary, the Mother of Jesus and our mother as well, and all the glorious hosts of heaven. We—whether on earth, in heaven, or in purgatory—are one Body in Christ. We all are branches grafted onto the same Vine. Christ's one sacrifice, which offers salvation to all, is present at every Mass for all time.

The Great Amen

All of the Eucharistic Prayers end with the same words:

Through him, and with him, and in him,
O God, almighty Father,
in the unity of the Holy Spirit,
all glory and honor is yours,
for ever and ever.

Borrowing terms from music, we would say that the Eucharistic Prayer has been a building crescendo. This prayer is the *denouement*—"the final resolution or clarification of a dramatic or narrative plot."[†] The priest and deacon hold the Body and Blood of Christ aloft for all to see, and the priest says the above prayer, which sums up the new reality gained for mankind in Christ. Christ has restored the order of creation and He has ratified a New Covenant in His Blood. Christ's sacrifice is a triumph over sin and death.

Our response to the work of the Trinity is the "Great Amen." We assent. Christ's work is done for all of creation and for each of us personally. In our individual "amens" we ask that it be so in our lives.

---

† Definition is from the American Heritage Dictionary of the English Language (Orlando, FL: Houghton Mifflin Company, 1992).

It is our personal and communal acknowledgement that there is only one Lord and Savior, Jesus Christ. He who is worshipped in heaven is at the same time really and truly present at our altar in the hands of His ministers. What an awe-filled reality we behold! He has shed His blood because of His mercy, in the power of the Holy Spirit, and for the glory of God the Father.

Communion and Concluding Rite (CCC 1355)

In some of the sacrifices of the Old Testament offered at the temple in Jerusalem, the people would eat part of what had been offered to God, as a sign of the covenant that bound God and man. These Old Testament sacrifices prefigure and find fulfillment in Jesus Christ. He is the sacrifice of the New Covenant. At every Mass we are witnesses of that one and only sacrifice of Calvary. God now will give Himself to us as Food.

We begin this rite by praying together the prayer that Christ taught His disciples. We acknowledge our Father "who art in heaven." We pray that His will be done and that our sins—our personal failures to implement His will—be forgiven. And we ask for the food that we most desperately need. Certainly, we need food to sustain the physical body, but our spiritual wellbeing is more important. In Christ we have salvation and the promise of eternal life. We need "the bread of heaven" and "the cup of salvation" (CCC 1355).

And what we ask of our Father, He does. He feeds us at Communion. The grace of the Sacrament is beyond all measure. Of course, its effect in our lives will depend on our response and our openness.

We do become what we eat. If we eat food high in fat, it will show in our waistlines. If we eat a healthy diet, it will show in our good physical health. If we worthily receive this heavenly food, we can become more Christ-like.

Recessional

Our Mass is now coming to an end. We have visited heaven and we have been fed with "the Bread of angels." As we leave, we recall that we gave our lives as part of the offering; we, too, were on the paten that was offered to the Father. We have received Christ not only for our own welfare, but so that we may become Christ. Therefore, we leave on mission to be, as divine bread, scattered to a needy world.

.

Liturgical Matters
That Do Matter

We have looked at an overview of the Mass. Let us now look more closely at how we can appreciate the Mass and participate more fully in it—how we can better focus our minds and hearts on God. Cardinal Joseph Ratzinger (now Pope Benedict XVI) wrote a wonderful book, *The Spirit of the Liturgy*, which can help us in our reflections.[*]

Participating in the Mass

Who performs the action of the Mass: a) the priest, b) the congregation, c) the individuals, d) God?

If you answered God, move to the head of the class! In *The Spirit of the Liturgy* Pope Benedict

---

[*] I highly recommend this book. It was translated into English by John Seward and published in 2000 by Ignatius Press.

writes, "The real 'action' in the liturgy . . . is the action of God himself. . . . God himself acts and does what is essential."[†]

God is always the initiator. He is the Creator. It is He who makes Himself accessible to us so that we can communicate with Him. He became man. His life, death, and Resurrection established the new creation, and He will come again at the end of time.

In the Mass God's action is seen most clearly during the Eucharistic Prayer. As the Consecration approaches, the human actor in the person of the priest steps back to make room for the *actio divina*, the action of God. We hear the voice of the priest, but he "speaks with the *I* of the Lord—'This is my Body,' 'This is my Blood.'"[‡]

Our active participation in Mass is cooperation with what God is doing. We offer ourselves, asking to be conformed to Christ and be transformed by Him—to "be made the true Body of Christ."[§] Pope Benedict encourages us that even our prayer of offering is already a participation in the sacrifice

---

† Joseph Cardinal Ratzinger, The Spirit of the Liturgy (San Francisco, Ignatius Press: 2000), 173.

‡ Ibid., 172.

§ Ibid., 173.

of Christ, for it is Christ who calls us to participate in His death and Resurrection.

Saint Paul writes in 1 Corinthians that when we are united to Christ we become "one spirit with him" (1 Cor. 6:17). Pope Benedict sees this reality in the Mass: "The point is that, ultimately, the difference between *actio Christi* [the action of Christ] and our own action is done away with. There is only *one* action, which is at the same time his and ours—ours because we have become 'one body and one spirit' with him. The uniqueness of the Eucharistic liturgy lies precisely in the fact that God himself is acting and that we are drawn into that action of God. Everything else is, therefore, secondary."¶

Reading and singing, standing and kneeling, processions and incense, bowing and giving the sign of peace all have a place at Mass. However, external actions are always secondary. "Doing" must be the outgrowth of something much more fundamental: giving ourselves to Christ and being transformed through that act of submitting.

It is vital that we surrender ourselves to the action of God because, as Pope Benedict writes, where His "will is done, there is heaven, there

¶ Ibid., 174.

earth becomes heaven." Our transformation in the Eucharist is to then bear fruit in the transformation of the world, for that which begins in the liturgy "is meant to unfold further beyond it." We are to carry to the world the "rule of love which is the Kingdom of God."**

So then, the "Go in peace" that ends the Mass is never a dismissal, but rather our marching orders.

Sacred Places

If you are married, you wouldn't use your wedding ring as a paint scraper. Why? Well, hopefully that ring represents something extremely important to you: a lifelong commitment of love to your spouse. That ring has been dedicated to a special purpose. It reminds you of a unique relationship, proclaims your commitment, and, in a real sense, makes your spouse present to you wherever you may be. We wouldn't be wrong to say that your wedding ring is "sacred."

The Code of Canon Law tells us that the Church is a "sacred place." It is a special place, "designated for divine worship" (canon 1210). The sacredness

** Ibid., 176.

of the place determines the design, the decoration, and the usage. Why do we strive to make the church a beautiful place? A clue can be found in the Old Testament. The Ark of the Covenant was kept in the innermost part of the Tent of Meeting. On the top of the Ark was the "mercy seat" surrounded by two angels (see Exodus 25:18). The seat and the angels were made of pure gold. Why so great an expense? Quite simply, that seat was reserved for God. It is true, as Pope Benedict has written, "The heavens cannot contain [God], but he has chosen the Ark as the 'footstool' of his presence."[††]

Later in history, the inner court of the temple in Jerusalem, the holy of holies, served a similar purpose. It was a place reserved for God's presence.

What of the Catholic church? Like the Ark and the temple, every Catholic church is set aside for God. What is more, the Lord of the universe is enthroned on our altars at and after the Consecration and continues to reside in the tabernacle. The Catholic Church far surpasses its antecedents in the Old Testament because Christ is truly present—Body and Blood, Soul and Divinity. Is it not

---

†† Ibid., 65.

right then to treat the church building as the sacred place it is?

The church building and its furnishings are also to help us worship. They are to point to Him whom we worship. In *The Spirit of the Liturgy*, Pope Benedict asks and answers the question about the importance of the church building and its décor. "Do we still need sacred space, sacred time, mediating symbols? Yes, we do need them, precisely so that, through the 'image,' through the sign, we learn to see the openness of heaven. We need them to give us the capacity to know the mystery of God . . . an entry into his representation that is an entry into reality itself. We do indeed participate in the heavenly liturgy, but this participation is mediated to us through earthly signs."[‡‡]

This understanding does have a personal component. Rightly we can ask ourselves: Does my clothing and demeanor in church reflect its sacred character, especially at Mass? Do I support my parish financially so that it may be a house of worship that reflects our service to God?

[‡‡] Ibid., 61.

Liturgy and Reality

When we think of what is real, images of bread, flowers, rocks, and other items that we can experience with our five senses come to mind. But, when we think more deeply about it, we realize that these "real" things are actually transitory. Bread will rot, flowers will die, and rocks will wear away.

At the core of our being we know that this world can't be all that there is. Creation, impressive as it is, points to something—Someone—greater. God has no beginning and no end. In Him is solid reality. Even though our five senses can't readily perceive Him, we nonetheless know that there is a God because, in multiple ways, He has revealed Himself to us.

The Catechism instructs us, "The world, and man, attest that they contain within themselves neither their first principle nor their final end, but rather that they participate in Being itself, which alone is without origin or end. Thus, in different ways, man can come to know that there exists a reality which is the first cause and final end of all things, a reality 'that everyone calls "God"' [St.

Thomas Aquinas, *Summa Theologica* 1, 2, 3]" (CCC 34).

In our very makeup we are wired to relate to God—to "participate in Being itself." What then is the *right* way to relate to God? In the only way that makes sense for the creature that stands before the Creator, we *worship*. Pope Benedict writes in *The Spirit of the Liturgy* that the Scriptures are the history of man learning to relate properly to God. In the Old Testament "Israel learns how to worship God in the way he himself desires."§§

Worship is not an ego trip for God. Instead, it is expression and experience of reality. There is a God, and He has a plan for our good. As Pope Benedict writes, "Worship, . . . the right way to relate to God, . . . has the character of anticipation. It lays hold in advance of a more perfect life and, in so doing, gives our life its proper measure."¶¶

The Mass is the perfect act of worship established by God Himself. In the liturgy we respond to God in the way that He has revealed to us. Each Mass is, as Pope Benedict indicates, "a kind of

---

§§ Ibid., 17.
¶¶ Ibid., 21.

anticipation, a rehearsal, a prelude for the life to come, for eternal life."***

At Mass we may feel distracted, hungry, sad, tired and any other number of feelings and sensations, but they are only transitory. At each Mass, the reality is that the eternal God gives Himself to us, and we have the opportunity to worship Him. In this we can examine ourselves: Do I judge a Mass "good" by the way I feel, or do I appreciate the reality that unfolds before me? Do I approach Mass as my opportunity to worship God?

At each Mass we can do that for which we were created. We relate to God and taste a little of eternity—a reality more firm than the chair on which you sit!

Our Bodies Participate in Worship

Stand, sing, sit, stand again, bow, sit again, stand, kneel. There are many actions and gestures during the course of a Mass. The liturgy fully involves us—mind, spirit, body—in this greatest of prayers. We have the opportunity to participate in a fully human way. And the gestures and actions of

*** Ibid., 14.

the Mass are to help us pray attentively. Ultimately, they aid us in loving God and receiving His love.

Let's reflect together.

There are no wasted expressions in the Mass. All of the actions are part of this great prayer. So how do the actions add to our prayer and draw us closer to God? Why do we do the things we do as Catholics at the Mass?

On Bended Knees

Body posture can speak louder than words. You can tell if a student is paying attention in class with just a glance at his posture. As we are flesh and spirit, our bodies can reveal our inner disposition and our disposition can dictate our physical posture.

In the Bible no one who recognizes God remains upright. From kings and prophets of Israel to John in the Book of Revelation, people fall to their knees or upon their faces in the presence of God. In fact, the word *kneeling* occurs twenty-four times in the Book of Revelation alone. Catholic scholars, including Pope Benedict, tell us that this final book of the Bible is really "the book of the heavenly liturgy, which is presented to the Church as the standard for her own liturgy."††† If kneeling is a right posture in heaven where the Lamb of God is enthroned, it is certainly appropriate at each and every Mass, where the Lamb that was slain is again presented to the Father and to us.

Jesus gives an example not only of this posture of prayer but also of the attitude it ought to manifest. In Saint Luke's Gospel we are told that during His agony on the Mount of Olives, Jesus knelt in prayer. His prayer while on his knees is instructive. Christ prays to His Father, "Not my will, but yours be done." Pope Benedict writes that Christ "lays [His] human will in the divine."‡‡‡ This conforming of the human will to the divine is at the heart of redemption, for the Fall of man was the exact opposite: man's will was put in opposition to the will of God. Adam and Eve rejected the command of God and rebelled. Pope Benedict tells us that those words—"Not my will, but yours"—are "the words of truth. . . . Only when our will rests in the will of God does it become truly will and truly free."§§§

---

††† Ibid., 85–186.
‡‡‡ Ibid., 187.
§§§ Ibid., 187.

We should strive to make this our attitude when we kneel at Mass.

Kneeling is also a sign of supplication and worship. The leper, asking to be healed, kneels before Jesus. When Jesus stills the waves, the disciples kneel before Him in the boat. And when the blind man acknowledges his belief, he does it from his knees. When we come before Christ at Mass or during a visit to the Blessed Sacrament, we too come in need of healing and redemption. We too are called to worship.

In the presence of Jesus "every knee should bow" (Phil. 2:10). Kneeling and genuflection are gestures that are reserved for God. When we genuflect, we reverence Jesus present in the tabernacle. We don't genuflect to the cross, to the altar, or to any other thing or person. We bend our knee to Jesus.

We are to kneel at two specific times during Mass. During the Consecration Jesus becomes present on the altar. In the United States we kneel from the Sanctus (Holy, Holy, Holy) until the Great Amen at the end of the Eucharistic Prayer. During this time a transformation occurs. Those gifts of simple bread and wine become the Body and Blood of the Second Person of the Trinity. That anticipated divine Guest arrives. We still see those elements of bread and wine, but Jesus is on the altar just as surely as we are in the pew. The correct response to mystery and miracle is wonder, awe, worship, and thanksgiving. Kneeling surely is the right posture for this moment of grace.

In the United States it is a pious custom to kneel after the recitation of the "Lamb of God." The priest elevates the Host to present our Lord, who now offers Himself to us as spiritual food. From our knees we rightly utter the words, "Lord, I am not worthy!" as we prepare ourselves to receive the Body and Blood of our Lord.

Standing at Attention

Standing is another important posture. When the principal walked into my grade school classroom, the teacher would announce: "Students, the principal is here." The students would rise from their seats and greet the headmaster. We would continue to stand until the teacher directed us to take our seats again.

The entry of the principal, or any dignitary, signaled that something special was about to happen. The routine was changed and our focus was altered. Standing was a sign of respect; we were at attention and anticipated what would come next.

The start of Mass is a time to stand; something important is about to happen. We need to be attentive and focused for we are expecting a special guest, the very Son of God. Our minds are to put aside distractions as we examine ourselves and seek forgiveness for our faults. And our hearts must turn to the One who has loved us to His very death.

There are other times during the Mass when we will be called to stand and be attentive. We stand for the Gospel, which is the high point of the Liturgy of the Word. The communal recitation of the Creed, our profession of faith, is another moment in the liturgy that demands something of us. We stand because our belief in these truths of the Creed is essential if we are to join with the fellowship of the faithful.

After the preparation of the altar and the presentation of the gifts, the priest addresses the congregation: "Pray brethren, that my sacrifice and yours may be acceptable to God . . ." This call to prayer requires our response. And so we who are offering our sacrifice stand and respond: "May the Lord accept the sacrifice."

Bowing before the King

Before receiving Communion we are asked to make a deep reverent bow. At Communion we approach a king—actually the King of kings! As the communicant approaches, the priest holds the Host up and proclaims the most powerful and earth-shaking words that can be uttered by man: this is "the Body of Christ." Our eyes see the appearance of bread, but our mind and our heart know more than our eyes can see. This is truly Jesus—this is no less than the Body of Christ. It is a mystery so profound that it demands a response. Before we receive, we will say our "Amen." In so doing we proclaim, "Yes, I perceive that this is Christ whom I am about to receive."

While Christ is offered to the person before us in the line, we bow because we behold our Lord, our King, and our God. Christ comes to us not only spiritually but physically. So as we prepare our heart and our mind, we also respond physically. We bow in reverence and in acknowledgement that our Savior is giving Himself to us.

Louder Than Words

Perhaps saying that our actions speak louder than our words is an overstatement. But surely our actions, when done out of devotion and with understanding, affirm our words and help us to pray.

Conclusion

We started this booklet with prayer and it seems most appropriate to end with prayer as well. It also is appropriate to draw from the great Doctor of the Church, Thomas Aquinas, whose hymns, prayers, and reflections on the Eucharist remain unmatched.

Prayer before Mass

Almighty and everlasting God,
behold, I come to the Sacrament
of Your only-begotten Son,
our Lord Jesus Christ.
I come as one infirm to the physician of life,
as one unclean to the fountain of mercy,
as one blind to the light
of everlasting brightness,
as one poor and needy to the Lord
of heaven and earth.
Therefore, I implore the abundance
of Your measureless bounty
that You would vouchsafe to
heal my infirmity,
wash my uncleanness,
enlighten my blindness,
enrich my poverty
and clothe my nakedness,
that I may receive the Bread of angels,
the King of kings,
the Lord of lords,
with such reverence and humility,
with such sorrow and devotion,

with such purity and faith,
with such purpose and intention
as may be profitable to my soul's salvation.
Grant unto me, I pray,
the grace of receiving not only the Sacrament
of our Lord's Body and Blood, but also
the grace and power of the Sacrament.
O most gracious God,
grant me so to receive
the Body of Your only-begotten Son,
our Lord Jesus Christ,
which He took from the Virgin Mary,
as to merit to be incorporated
into His mystical Body,
and to be numbered among His members.
O most loving Father,
give me grace to behold forever
Your beloved Son
with His face at last unveiled,
whom I now propose to receive
under the sacramental veil here below.
Amen.

—Saint Thomas Aquinas

Thanksgiving after Communion

I give You thanks, O holy Lord,
Father Almighty, Eternal God,
that You have vouchsafed,
for no merit of my own,
but of the mere condescension of Your mercy,
to satisfy me, a sinner
and Your unworthy servant,
with the Precious Blood of Your Son
our Lord Jesus Christ.
I implore You,
let not this Holy Communion be to me
an increase of guilt unto my punishment,
but an availing plea
unto pardon and forgiveness.
Let it be to me the armor of faith
and the shield of good will.
Grant that it may work
the extinction of my vices,
the rooting out of concupiscence and lust,
and the increase within me
of charity and patience,
of humility and obedience.

Let it be my strong defense
against the snares of all my enemies,
visible and invisible;
the stilling and the calm of all my impulses,
carnal and spiritual;
my indissoluble union with You
the one and true God,
and a blessed consummation at my last end.
And I beseech You
that You would vouchsafe to bring me,
sinner as I am,
to that ineffable banquet where You,
with the Son and the Holy Ghost,
are to Your saints true and unfailing light,
fullness and content,
joy for evermore,
gladness without alloy,
consummate and everlasting bliss.
Through the same Jesus Christ our Lord
Amen.

—*Saint Thomas Aquinas*

From the hymn "Lauda Sion"

Thus in faith the Christian heareth:
That Christ's Flesh as bread appeareth,
    And as wine His Precious Blood:
Though we feel it not nor see it,
Living Faith that doth decree it
    All defects of sense makes good.
Lo! beneath the species dual
(Signs not things), is hid a jewel
    Far beyond creation's reach!
Though His Flesh as food abideth,
And His Blood as drink–He hideth
    Undivided under each.

—Saint Thomas Aquinas,
trans. H. T. Henry

The Faith Basics Series

- Death, Where Is Your Sting? A Catholic Approach to Death

- Come to the Celebration: The Church's Liturgical Year

- Prayer: A Catholic Perspective

- Sacramentals and Signs: Objects, Actions, and Words as Avenues for Grace

- Sacraments: The Seven Spiritual Wonders of the World

- Discovering the "Awe" of the Mass